Tomfoolery!

RANDOLPH CALDECOTT

and the

RAMBUNCTIOUS COMING-of-AGE

of CHILDREN'S BOOKS

written by

Michelle Markel

illustrated by

Barbara McClintock

chronicle books · san francisco

Come on in.

A whole world lives and breathes inside these pages. You'll find *frisky animals*, *sprightly characters*, and *a hero* so chipper he can barely hold still on the paper.

BUT IN THE 1850S, there are no children's books like this one. Many are published, but their pictures look stiff, full of pretty poses and cluttered scenery. No one has yet imagined how much fun an illustrated book could be.

No one, until . . .

OF THE MILL.

And there was a king, who was
not a good man, and no one thought
... him; for no one likes bad men.
... his king went one day to
... wood, and in his way
... had to pass the mill
... good man dwelt: and as
... the mill, he said to the
... who were with him, Whose

FRONTISPIECE.

Quick!

If you don't move fast, you're going to miss him—
RANDOLPH CALDECOTT, future famous illustrator.

A fever has weakened his heart and left him frail,

but he loves to be outdoors . . .

Oh, there he is, strolling down the country lane,

watching his favorite things in the whole world—animals:

ducks geese dogs sheep cows pigs hens horses!

As soon as he gets home, Randolph grabs a pencil,

and they rush across his paper:

Trotting!

Tumbling!

Leaping!

Waddling!

It is too much fun. It cannot be helped. It can happen anytime
he has something to draw on—even in his schoolbooks.

Randolph's father doesn't approve of this artwork.
When his son turns 15, he sends Randolph to work at the most sensible
place he can think of—a bank.

But the lad has loads of time for horseback rides and hunting meets—
though he gets out of breath. Best of all, he has time to draw. One day
he sketches a fire blazing through the railway hotel . . . and a famous
newspaper publishes it!

Randolph has the sneaking feeling he could earn a living
by selling pictures. He gets a job at another bank, in a bigger city,
where many artists live.

There he is—the handsome chap at the wooden desk.

WHAT'S HE DOING WITH THAT PEN?

Instead of working sums, he's doodling donkey heads! On bank stationery!

Randolph doesn't worry. The lads at work like his jokes and the witty pictures he makes for them.

So do the editors he meets at a club.

Before long, Randolph sells his drawings to a well-known magazine. He's got money in his pockets and hope in his heart.

Goodbye, Manchester!

SO MANY PEOPLE, SO MANY SIGHTS, SO MUCH TO SKETCH FOR THE NEWSPAPERS!

Randolph goes to sessions of Parliament, to fashionable weddings, to boat races on the river, where he gets squashed in the squishingest crowds he's ever seen.

But at night, alone in his workshop,
he misses his friends.
He misses living in the country.
Sometimes, on his letters, he draws
himself as a sad, frumpled cartoon.

Randolph wants to be the best artist
he can be. He's not as skilled as the famous
illustrators, painters, and sculptors
he meets—people who've studied in fine
academies, in Paris.

Could he ever do the kinds
of things they do?

He tries. Randolph illustrates his first travel book. Instead of scenic mountains, he draws the action—that row of school kids and a poodle as they march off on tour.

Randolph starts making home decor. Does he paint fruit stuck in a bowl? No, he studies storks at the zoological gardens, then paints them lifting off in flight.

A famous French sculptor teaches him to model with clay, and Randolph pays him with English lessons. But he doesn't sculpt ladies in pretty poses—he sculpts hunters on the chase of wild boars,

a cat about to
pounce!

Now reader, our hero's too weak to be
painting sculpting illustrating reporting
on balloon launches,

elections, expositions;

traveling in the

wind and rain;

working long through the night;
inking in every whisker, boot,
and button.

He ends up exhausted in bed.

The doctors tell him to take it easy—but Randolph can't hold still for long. And all his projects are making him a better artist! What gets the most notice are his illustrations—especially for books. An actor *lunging*, a swell *strutting*, a cocky coachman *flinging* a whip. Randolph's pen-and-ink people *burst* with personality. They *jitter* with life.

Someone pays close attention to those pictures. Someone who's printed several books of illustrated alphabets, songs, and nursery rhymes. The finest color printer in London!

One day he calls on Randolph with an offer. Can you guess what it is?

"Would you like to make some picture books?"

Picture books! For tots! That's a brand-new audience for Randolph.

He's seen the books at shops and railway stalls. The pictures don't move the stories forward—they're like ornate decorations.

Still . . . Randolph has no kids, but he likes what kids like—*action!* And he loves what kids love—*animals!*

He knows just what to do.

He dips his nib in the ink . . .

and **TALLYHO!**

A rat *darts* across the storehouse,
pops up in the floorboards,
jumps upon a pot . . .

a cat *crouches*,

a cow *charges!*

No frilly lines,

no fussy backgrounds,

no crowded pages—

scene by scene the story tumbles forth like life.

A horse hurtles down the lane with Mr. Gilpin.

Off goes the hat!

Off flies the wig!

No words on the page, but you can almost hear the hoofbeats—
clompety clompety clomp!

The drawings sweep through the stories with a glee and gusto
never seen before.

The printer chooses the best inks, the most skilled

hands to engrave the illustrations, and . . .

The public is delighted! The critics are astonished.

Randolph Caldecott—**WHAT HAS HE DONE?**

28

He has poured joy into his characters. He has built entire worlds for them to romp through. He has given children stories in pictures they can understand, even if they haven't yet learned to read.

For several years, Randolph's natty frogs, his queen of hearts, his mousies in muslin, and his runaway spoons and dishes hop and dance through thousands of nurseries. He becomes an international success.

ANNOTATIONS

Pages 5–7
Randolph Caldecott was born on March 22, 1846, in the market town of Chester, England, where his father had a business. The family lived upstairs from his shop.

Young Randolph drew, painted, modeled from clay, and carved wooden animals. Although a bout of rheumatic fever left him frail, he loved to ramble in the countryside.

Pages 8–9
Caldecott left school at the age of 14, like many boys of his social background. In 1861, he moved to the town of Whitchurch to work as a bank clerk, lodging in the farmhouse of a couple who lived nearby. Much of the rustic scenery he saw during this period appears in his later drawings.

Caldecott's sketch of a fire that nearly destroyed the Queen Railway Hotel was published in the *Illustrated London News*, a popular newspaper.

Pages 10–11
After moving to Manchester in 1867, Caldecott took night classes in art and made useful contacts at the Brasenose Club, a center for the city's artistic community. He was published in local magazines and was later put in touch with Thomas Armstrong, the artist who submitted Caldecott's drawings to *London Society*. Armstrong and the magazine's editor, Henry Blackburn, became two of Caldecott's closest friends.

Pages 12–13
In 1872, Caldecott moved into an apartment across from the British Museum in London. He sold a drawing to *Punch*, a humorous magazine, and later to the *Graphic*, a popular weekly newspaper.

Pages 14–15
Caldecott visited the countryside as often as his busy schedule allowed.

In a letter to a friend, he wrote:

> Wasn't Sunday a glorious day! I communed alone during the morning in a pine wood. I would describe it, but if you go into a pine wood and open your eyes, ears and nose and take off your hat as the sun glances down through the tree tops, making the insects to hum and the perfume to spread, why, you will save me trying to do what I cannot.

Page 16
Caldecott's first commissioned book illustrations were made for Blackburn's *The Harz Mountains: A Tour in the Toy Country* (1873). According to the editor, Caldecott used a German phrase book to communicate with the villagers, speaking slowly so he could study their faces.

On his own, and in collaboration with Armstrong, Caldecott made decorative art for the homes of wealthy clients. Birds were a favorite subject. Besides storks, Caldecott painted swans, pigeons, and pelicans.

ILLUSTRATED VICTORIAN PERIODICALS

When Randolph Caldecott moved to London, there was a huge market for illustrated newspapers and magazines. Some of them published realistic drawings of catastrophes and other current events, while others specialized in gently humorous scenes of daily life and political cartoons. Many celebrated artists contributed to the periodicals, including George Cruikshank, who illustrated works by Charles Dickens, and John Tenniel, who made pictures for Lewis Carroll's Alice books.

The artists drew their pictures on woodblocks, which were then sent to engraving workshops. One of the engravers was Edmund Evans, who became a talented printer of color illustrated books—including those of Randolph Caldecott.

TOY BOOK ILLUSTRATORS: THE BIG THREE

In the 1860s, most picture books for children, called "toy books," were cheaply produced and crudely illustrated. Evans wanted to make toy books that were as beautiful as illustrated books for adults—which had become popular gift items. In 1865, he and artist Walter Crane began to produce a series of elegant, brilliantly colored, and richly decorated picture books. Published by Warne, then Routledge, the six-page sixpenny books were highly successful. Parents saw Crane's tasteful picture books as a way to introduce art to their children.

When Crane chose to stop making toy books, Evans hired Caldecott as his successor. Caldecott was allowed to experiment with the format and to bring his own vision to the traditional material—fairy tales, songs, poems, and popular stories.

A reviewer in the *Times* (1878) said,

> In a few strokes, dashed off apparently at random, he can portray a scene or incident to the full as correctly and completely and far more lucidly than Mr. Crane in his later and far more elaborate style.

A year after publishing Caldecott's first books, Evans launched the career of Kate Greenaway, whose father he had known in the engraving business. Though Greenaway's pictures were set in an England of earlier times, like Crane's and Caldecott's, her style was quaint and delicate, featuring children who looked like porcelain dolls. During the 1880s, Evans went on to publish two or three of Greenaway's books each year.

Caldecott was friendly with the other two artists. In his memoir, Crane recalled that Caldecott used to ride over on horseback in the early evening so he could play with Crane's children before bedtime. Caldecott and Greenaway corresponded and used some of the same models.

BIBLIOGRAPHY

Books

Alderson, Brian. *Sing a Song for Sixpence: The English Picture Book Tradition and Randolph Caldecott.* London: Cambridge University Press in association with the British Library, 1986.

Billington, Elizabeth T., ed. *The Randolph Caldecott Treasury.* New York: Frederick Warne, 1978.

Blackburn, Henry. *Randolph Caldecott: A Personal Memoir of His Early Art Career.* London: Sampson Low, Marston, Searle, and Rivington, 1886.

Darton, F. J. Harvey. *Children's Books in England: Five Centuries of Social Life.* 3rd ed. Revised by Brian Alderson. Cambridge: Cambridge University Press, 1982.

Davis, Mary Gould. *Randolph Caldecott, 1846–1886: An Appreciation.* Philadelphia: J. B. Lippincott, 1946.

Engen, Rodney K. *Randolph Caldecott: "Lord of the Nursery."* London: Bloomsbury, 1976.

Hutchins, Michael, ed. *Yours Pictorially: Illustrated Letters of Randolph Caldecott.* London: Frederick Warne, 1976.

Lundin, Anne H. *Victorian Horizons: The Reception of the Picture Books of Walter Crane, Randolph Caldecott, and Kate Greenaway.* Lanham, MD: Children's Literature Association and Scarecrow Press, 2001.

Whalley, Joyce Irene, and Tessa Rose Chester. *A History of Children's Book Illustration.* London: John Murray with the Victoria and Albert Museum, 1988.

Articles

Avery, Gillian. "Caldecott and the English Picture Book Tradition." *Children's Literature* 18 (1990): 169–72.

Cech, John. "Remembering Caldecott: *The Three Jovial Huntsmen* and the Art of the Picture Book." *The Lion and the Unicorn* 7/8 (1983–84): 110–19.

Landes, Sonia. "Picture Books as Literature." *Children's Literature Association Quarterly* 10, no. 2 (Summer 1985): 51–54.

May, Jill P. "Illustrations in Children's Books." *Children's Literature Association Quarterly* 6, no. 4 (Winter 1981): 17–21.

McNair, John R. "Chromolithography and Color Woodblock: Handmaidens to Nineteenth-Century Children's Literature." *Children's Literature Association Quarterly* 11, no. 4 (Winter 1986–87): 193–97.

Mirel, Barbara. "Tradition and the Individual Retelling." *Children's Literature Association Quarterly* 9, no. 2 (Summer 1984): 63–66.

Op de Beeck, Nathalie. "Suspended Animation: Picture Book Storytelling, Twentieth-Century Childhood, and William Nicholson's *Clever Bill.*" *The Lion and the Unicorn* 30, no. 1 (2006): 54–75.

Schiller, Justin G. "Artistic Awareness in Early Children's Books." *Children's Literature* 3 (1974): 177–85.